Design

2005 TASCHEN DIARY

www.taschen.com

09–12.2004

SEPTEMBER

1	We
2	Th
3	Fr
4	Sa
5	Su

WEEK 37

6	Mo ☽
7	Tu
8	We
9	Th
10	Fr
11	Sa
12	Su

WEEK 38

13	Mo
14	Tu ●
15	We
16	Th
17	Fr
18	Sa
19	Su

WEEK 39

20	Mo
21	Tu ◑
22	We
23	Th
24	Fr
25	Sa
26	Su

WEEK 40

27	Mo
28	Tu ○
29	We
30	Th

OCTOBER

1	Fr
2	Sa
3	Su

WEEK 41

4	Mo
5	Tu
6	We ☽
7	Th
8	Fr
9	Sa
10	Su

WEEK 42

11	Mo
12	Tu
13	We
14	Th ●
15	Fr
16	Sa
17	Su

WEEK 43

18	Mo
19	Tu
20	We ◑
21	Th
22	Fr
23	Sa
24	Su

WEEK 44

25	Mo
26	Tu
27	We
28	Th ○
29	Fr
30	Sa
31	Su

NOVEMBER

WEEK 45

1	Mo
2	Tu
3	We
4	Th
5	Fr ☽
6	Sa
7	Su

WEEK 46

8	Mo
9	Tu
10	We
11	Th
12	Fr ●
13	Sa
14	Su

WEEK 47

15	Mo
16	Tu
17	We
18	Th
19	Fr ◑
20	Sa
21	Su

WEEK 48

22	Mo
23	Tu
24	We
25	Th
26	Fr ○
27	Sa
28	Su

WEEK 49

29	Mo
30	Tu

DECEMBER

1	We
2	Th
3	Fr
4	Sa
5	Su ☽

WEEK 50

6	Mo
7	Tu
8	We
9	Th
10	Fr
11	Sa
12	Su ●

WEEK 51

13	Mo
14	Tu
15	We
16	Th
17	Fr
18	Sa ◑
19	Su

WEEK 52

20	Mo
21	Tu
22	We
23	Th
24	Fr
25	Sa
26	Su ○

WEEK 53

27	Mo
28	Tu
29	We
30	Th
31	Fr

01–04.2005

JANUARY	FEBRUARY	MARCH	APRIL
1 Sa	1 Tu	1 Tu	1 Fr
2 Su	2 We ☽	2 We	2 Sa ☽
WEEK 1	3 Th	3 Th ☽	3 Su
3 Mo ☽	4 Fr	4 Fr	**WEEK 14**
4 Tu	5 Sa	5 Sa	4 Mo
5 We	6 Su	6 Su	5 Tu
6 Th	**WEEK 6**	**WEEK 10**	6 We
7 Fr	7 Mo	7 Mo	7 Th
8 Sa	8 Tu ●	8 Tu	8 Fr ●
9 Su	9 We	9 We	9 Sa
WEEK 2	10 Th	10 Th ●	10 Su
10 Mo ●	11 Fr	11 Fr	**WEEK 15**
11 Tu	12 Sa	12 Sa	11 Mo
12 We	13 Su	13 Su	12 Tu
13 Th	**WEEK 7**	**WEEK 11**	13 We
14 Fr	14 Mo	14 Mo	14 Th
15 Sa	15 Tu	15 Tu	15 Fr
16 Su	16 We ◐	16 We	16 Sa ◐
WEEK 3	17 Th	17 Th ◐	17 Su
17 Mo ◐	18 Fr	18 Fr	**WEEK 16**
18 Tu	19 Sa	19 Sa	18 Mo
19 We	20 Su	20 Su	19 Tu
20 Th	**WEEK 8**	**WEEK 12**	20 We
21 Fr	21 Mo	21 Mo	21 Th
22 Sa	22 Tu	22 Tu	22 Fr
23 Su	23 We	23 We	23 Sa
WEEK 4	24 Th ○	24 Th	24 Su ○
24 Mo	25 Fr	25 Fr ○	**WEEK 17**
25 Tu ○	26 Sa	26 Sa	25 Mo
26 We	27 Su	27 Su	26 Tu
27 Th	**WEEK 9**	**WEEK 13**	27 We
28 Fr	28 Mo	28 Mo	28 Th
29 Sa		29 Tu	29 Fr
30 Su		30 We	30 Sa
WEEK 5		31 Th	
31 Mo			

05–08.2005

MAY	JUNE	JULY	AUGUST
1 Su ☽	1 We	1 Fr	**WEEK 31**
WEEK 18	2 Th	2 Sa	1 Mo
2 Mo	3 Fr	3 Su	2 Tu
3 Tu	4 Sa	**WEEK 27**	3 We
4 We	5 Su	4 Mo	4 Th
5 Th	**WEEK 23**	5 Tu	5 Fr ●
6 Fr	6 Mo ●	6 We ●	6 Sa
7 Sa	7 Tu	7 Th	7 Su
8 Su ●	8 We	8 Fr	**WEEK 32**
WEEK 19	9 Th	9 Sa	8 Mo
9 Mo	10 Fr	10 Su	9 Tu
10 Tu	11 Sa	**WEEK 28**	10 We
11 We	12 Su	11 Mo	11 Th
12 Th	**WEEK 24**	12 Tu	12 Fr
13 Fr	13 Mo	13 We	13 Sa ☾
14 Sa	14 Tu	14 Th ☾	14 Su
15 Su	15 We ☾	15 Fr	**WEEK 33**
WEEK 20	16 Th	16 Sa	15 Mo
16 Mo ☾	17 Fr	17 Su	16 Tu
17 Tu	18 Sa	**WEEK 29**	17 We
18 We	19 Su	18 Mo	18 Th
19 Th	**WEEK 25**	19 Tu	19 Fr ○
20 Fr	20 Mo	20 We	20 Sa
21 Sa	21 Tu	21 Th ○	21 Su
22 Su	22 We ○	22 Fr	**WEEK 34**
WEEK 21	23 Th	23 Sa	22 Mo
23 Mo ○	24 Fr	24 Su	23 Tu
24 Tu	25 Sa	**WEEK 30**	24 We
25 We	26 Su	25 Mo	25 Th
26 Th	**WEEK 26**	26 Tu	26 Fr ☽
27 Fr	27 Mo	27 We	27 Sa
28 Sa	28 Tu ☽	28 Th ☽	28 Su
29 Su	29 We	29 Fr	**WEEK 35**
WEEK 22	30 Th	30 Sa	29 Mo
30 Mo ☽		31 Su	30 Tu
31 Tu			31 We

09–12.2005

SEPTEMBER	OCTOBER	NOVEMBER	DECEMBER
1 Th	1 Sa	1 Tu	1 Th ●
2 Fr	2 Su	2 We ●	2 Fr
3 Sa ●	**WEEK 40**	3 Th	3 Sa
4 Su	3 Mo ●	4 Fr	4 Su
WEEK 36	4 Tu	5 Sa	**WEEK 49**
5 Mo	5 We	6 Su	5 Mo
6 Tu	6 Th	**WEEK 45**	6 Tu
7 We	7 Fr	7 Mo	7 We
8 Th	8 Sa	8 Tu	8 Th ◐
9 Fr	9 Su	9 We ◑	9 Fr
10 Sa	**WEEK 41**	10 Th	10 Sa
11 Su ◑	10 Mo ◑	11 Fr	11 Su
WEEK 37	11 Tu	12 Sa	**WEEK 50**
12 Mo	12 We	13 Su	12 Mo
13 Tu	13 Th	**WEEK 46**	13 Tu
14 We	14 Fr	14 Mo	14 We
15 Th	15 Sa	15 Tu	15 Th ○
16 Fr	16 Su	16 We ○	16 Fr
17 Sa	**WEEK 42**	17 Th	17 Sa
18 Su ○	17 Mo ○	18 Fr	18 Su
WEEK 38	18 Tu	19 Sa	**WEEK 51**
19 Mo	19 We	20 Su	19 Mo
20 Tu	20 Th	**WEEK 47**	20 Tu
21 We	21 Fr	21 Mo	21 We
22 Th	22 Sa	22 Tu	22 Th
23 Fr	23 Su	23 We ◑	23 Fr ◑
24 Sa	**WEEK 43**	24 Th	24 Sa
25 Su ◑	24 Mo	25 Fr	25 Su
WEEK 39	25 Tu ◑	26 Sa	**WEEK 52**
26 Mo	26 We	27 Su	26 Mo
27 Tu	27 Th	**WEEK 48**	27 Tu
28 We	28 Fr	28 Mo	28 We
29 Th	29 Sa	29 Tu	29 Th
30 Fr	30 Su	30 We	30 Fr
	WEEK 44		31 Sa ●
	31 Mo		

CREDITS

p. 3: **Björn Dahlström**, *Rocking Bunny* children's toy for Playsam, 1985

p. 4: **Stefano Giovannoni**, *Volcano* watch for Alba-Seiko, 1998

Week 53: **Hugo Blomberg, Ralph Lysell & Gösta Thames**, *Ericofon* telephone, 1954 – launched in 1956

Week 1: **Eero Aarnio**, *Pastilli* chair for Asko, 1967

Week 2: **Ross Lovegrove**, *Aircraft seat* for Japan Airlines, 2000

Week 3: **Arne Jacobsen**, *Model no. 3316 Egg* chair for Fritz Hansen, 1958

Week 4: **Jens Quistgaard**, teak icebucket for Dansk International Designs, 1960

Week 5: **James Dyson**, *CRO1* Contrarotator two-drum washing machine for Dyson, 1996–2000

Week 6: **Jørgen Høvelskov**, *Harp* chair for Christensen & Larsen, 1968

Week 7: **Gunnel Nyman**, cased glass vases and *Pearl Necklace* vase for Nuutajärvi, 1947 & c. 1950

Week 8: **Kay Bojesen**, *Puffin* toy, Kay Bojesen's workshop, 1954

Week 9: **Elephant Design**, *Cigarro* personal computer, 2000

Week 10: **Eero Aarnio**, armchair for Asko, c. 1967

Week 11: **Gaetano Pesce**, Up Series for C & B Italia (later B & B Italia), 1969

Week 12: **Verner Panton**, *Kugel-Lampem TYP F (Ball lamp)* hanging lamp for J. Lüber, 1969 – produced from 1970

Week 13: **Charles & Ray Eames**, Prototype of the *LCW* chair, c. 1945

Week 14: **Charles & Ray Eames**, *DAR* chair for Zenith Plastics and later for Herman Miller, 1948–1950

Week 15: **Carl-Arne Breger**, *Ericofon 700* telephone for Ericsson, 1976

Week 16: **Jens Quistgaard**, *Fjord* cutlery for Dansk International Designs, 1953

Week 17: **Verner Panton**, *Phantasy Landscape* for *Visiona II* exhibition by Bayer AG at the Cologne Furniture Fair, 1970

Week 18: **Tapio Wirkkala**, double-headed cased glass vases for Iittala, 1955–1956

Week 19: **Naoto Fukasawa**, *Without thought* cd player for DMN, as part of *Without Thought* project, 1990

Week 20: t: **Jonathan Ive**, *iSub* sub-woofer for Harman Kardon, 1999 b: *Power Mac G4* computer for Apple Computer, 1999

Week 21: **Gocken Jobs**, *Trollslända (Dragonfly)* textile manufactured by Jobs Workshop for Ljungbergs Textiltryck, 1945

Week 22: **Poul Henningsen**, *PH Artichoke* lamp for Louis Poulsen, 1957

Week 23: **Hochschule für Gestaltung, Ulm**, *Exporter 2* portable radio for Braun, 1956

Week 24: **Christophe Pillet**, saucepan for the *Pots and Pans* microwave experimental project for Whirlpool, 2000

Week 25: **Poul Kjærholm**, *PK9* chair for Fritz Hansen, 1960

Week 26: **Ross Lovegrove**, *Solar Seed* – product architecture concept for a wholly autonomous nomadic structure, 1999

Week 27: **Philippe Starck**, *Attila* stool-table for Kartell, 1999

Week 28: **Ingo Maurer**, *XXL Dome* pendant lamps in Westfriedhof subway station, Munich, 1999

Week 29: **Arne Jacobsen**, *Model No. 3107 – Series 7* chair for Fritz Hansen, 1952

Week 30: **Poul Kjærholm**, *Model no. PK22* chair for F. Kold Christensen, 1955 – reissued by Fritz Hansen

Week 31: **Philippe Starck**, *TeddyBearBand* toy for Moulin Roty, 1998

Week 32: **Jasper Morrison**, *Bird-Table* for Magis, 2000

Week 33: **Verner Panton**, *VP-Globe* lamp for Louis Poulsen, 1969

Week 34: **Poul Volther**, *Model no. EJ 605 Corona* chair for Erik Jørgensen, 1961

Week 35: **Jasper Morrison**, *Air-Chair* for Magis, 1999

Week 36: tl: **Marc Newson**, *Orgone* plastic chair for Pod, 1998 tr: **Marc Newson**, *Bath Plug* for Alessi, 1997 b: **Marc Newson**, *David Gill* chair for B&B Italia, 1998

Week 37: **Marcello Nizzoli**, *Mirella* sewing machine for Necchi, 1957

Week 38: **Philippe Starck**, *StarckNaked* seamless tubular garment with integrated pantihose for Wolford, 1998

Week 39: Marianne Panton seated on a Panton chair with matching table, c. 1970

Week 40: **Harri Koskinen**, *Atlas* candle-holder & vase for Iittala, 1996

Week 41: **Josef Frank**, *Dixieland* textile for Svenskt Tenn, 1943–1944

Week 42: **Ingegerd Råman**, *Skyline* vases for Orrefors, 2000

Week 43: **Nick Crosbie**, *Lounge chair* for Inflate, 1997

Week 44: **Vilhelm Wohlert**, *Satellite* pendant lamp for Louis Poulsen, 1959

Week 45: **Olavi Lindén**, *Clippers* garden tools for Fiskars, 1996

Week 46: **Finn Juhl**, *Chieftain* chair for Niels Vodder, 1949

Week 47: **Tapio Wirkkala**, *Model no. 66-057* hanging lamp produced by Iittala for Stockmann, 1961

Week 48: **Carl-Arne Breger**, stoneware water jug for Gustavsberg, 1957–1958

Week 49: **Alvar Aalto**, *Model no. 60* stool for Artek, 1932–1933

Week 50: **Ettore Sottsass**, *Carlton* shelf unit for Memphis, 1981

Week 51: **Sigvard Bernadotte & Acton Bjørn**, *Margrethe* melamine mixing bowls for Rosti, 1950

Week 52: **Sam Hecht**, *NTT Docomo* phone for Electrotextiles, 2000

Last page: **Tapio Wirkkala**, laminated birch platter executed by Martti Lindqvist, 1951

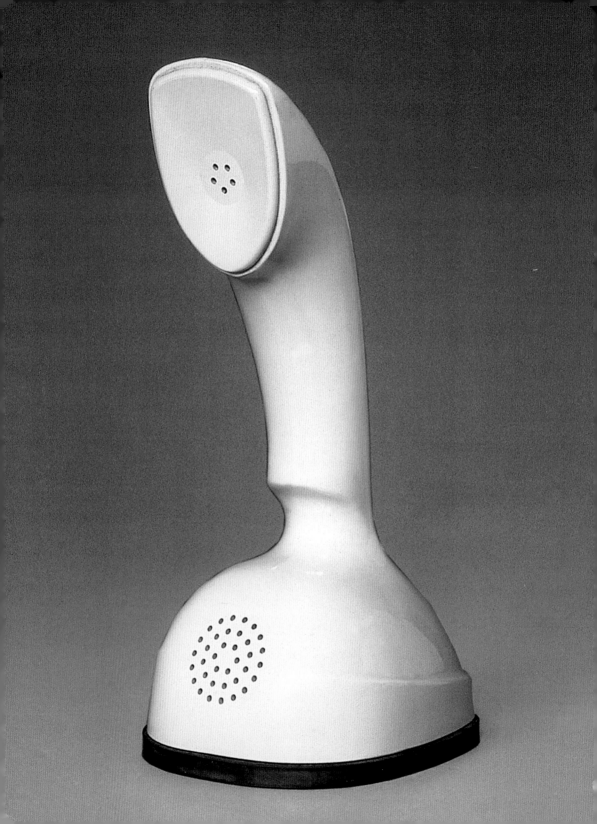

53. WEEK

12.2004 | 01.2005

Monday Montag Lundi Lunes Lunedì Segunda-feira Maandag 月

27

Tuesday Dienstag Mardi Martes Martedì Terça-feira Dinsdag 火

28

Wednesday Mittwoch Mercredi Miércoles Mercoledì Quarta-feira Woensdag 水

29

Thursday Donnerstag Jeudi Jueves Giovedì Quinta-feira Donderdag 木

30

Friday Freitag Vendredi Viernes Venerdì Sexta-feira Vrijdag 金

31

Saturday Samstag Samedi Sábado Sabato Sábado Zaterdag 土

1

New Year's Day | Jour de l'An |
Nouvel An | Neujahr | Capodanno |
Nieuwjaarsdag | Año Nuevo | Ano Novo

Sunday Sonntag Dimanche Domingo Domenica Domingo Zondag 日

2

1. WEEK

01.2005

Monday	3	10	17	24	31
Tuesday	4	11	18	25	1
Wednesday	5	12	19	26	2
Thursday	6	13	20	27	3
Friday	7	14	21	28	4
Saturday	8	15	22	29	5
Sunday	9	16	23	30	6
WEEK	1	2	3	4	5

Monday Montag Lundi Lunes Lunedì Segunda-feira Maandag 月

(UK) (CDN)

Public Holiday | Jour Férié

3

Tuesday Dienstag Mardi Martes Martedì Terça-feira Dinsdag 火

(UK) Public Holiday (Scotland only)

4

Wednesday Mittwoch Mercredi Miércoles Mercoledì Quarta-feira Woensdag 水

5

Thursday Donnerstag Jeudi Jueves Giovedì Quinta-feira Donderdag 木

(D) Heilige Drei Könige (teilweise)

(A) (E) (I) Heilige Drei Könige |

Reyes | Epifania

6

Friday Freitag Vendredi Viernes Venerdì Sexta-feira Vrijdag 金

7

Saturday Samstag Samedi Sábado Sabato Sábado Zaterdag 土

8

Sunday Sonntag Dimanche Domingo Domenica Domingo Zondag 日

9

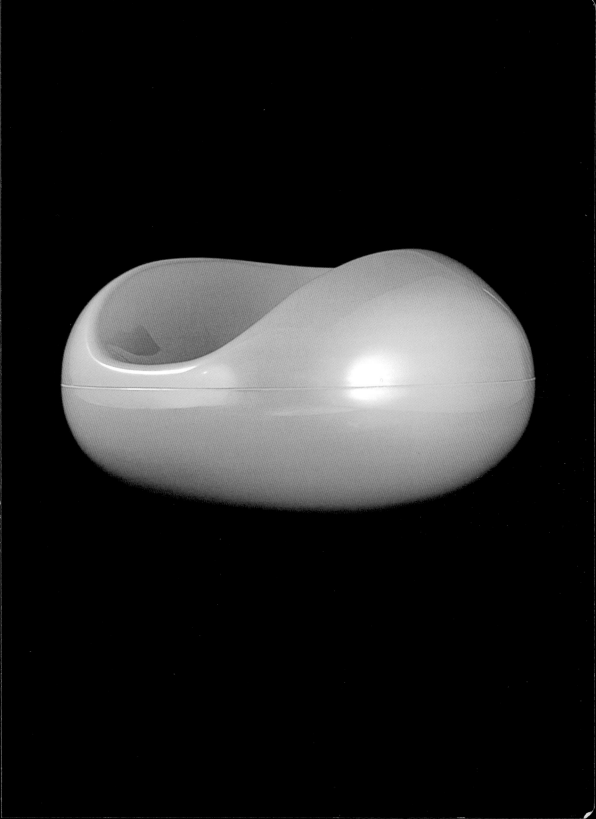

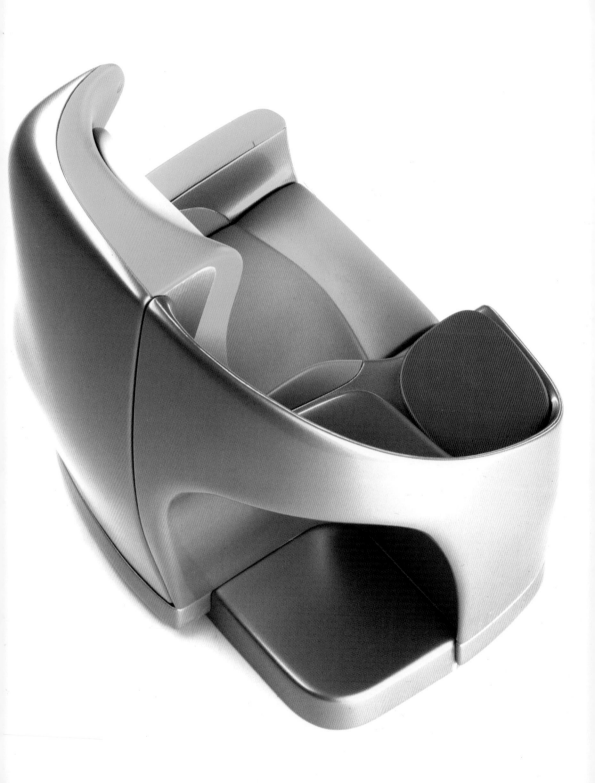

2. WEEK

01.2005

Monday Montag Lundi Lunes Lunedì Segunda-feira Maandag 月

●   (J) Coming-of-Age Day

10

Tuesday Dienstag Mardi Martes Martedì Terça-feira Dinsdag 火

11

Wednesday Mittwoch Mercredi Miércoles Mercoledì Quarta-feira Woensdag 水

12

Thursday Donnerstag Jeudi Jueves Giovedì Quinta-feira Donderdag 木

13

Friday Freitag Vendredi Viernes Venerdì Sexta-feira Vrijdag 金

14

Saturday Samstag Samedi Sábado Sabato Sábado Zaterdag 土

15

Sunday Sonntag Dimanche Domingo Domenica Domingo Zondag 日

16

3. WEEK

Monday	17	24	31	7	14
Tuesday	18	25	1	8	15
Wednesday	19	26	2	9	16
Thursday	20	27	3	10	17
Friday	21	28	4	11	18
Saturday	22	29	5	12	19
Sunday	23	30	6	13	20
WEEK	**3**	**4**	**5**	**6**	**7**

Monday Montag Lundi Lunes Lunedì Segunda-feira Maandag 月

◐   (USA) Martin Luther King Day

17

Tuesday Dienstag Mardi Martes Martedì Terça-feira Dinsdag 火

18

Wednesday Mittwoch Mercredi Miércoles Mercoledì Quarta-feira Woensdag 水

19

Thursday Donnerstag Jeudi Jueves Giovedì Quinta-feira Donderdag 木

20

Friday Freitag Vendredi Viernes Venerdì Sexta-feira Vrijdag 金

21

Saturday Samstag Samedi Sábado Sabato Sábado Zaterdag 土

22

Sunday Sonntag Dimanche Domingo Domenica Domingo Zondag 日

23

4. WEEK

01.2005

Monday	24	31	7	14	21
Tuesday	25	1	8	15	22
Wednesday	26	2	9	16	23
Thursday	27	3	10	17	24
Friday	28	4	11	18	25
Saturday	29	5	12	19	26
Sunday	30	6	13	20	27
WEEK	4	5	6	7	8

Monday Montag Lundi Lunes Lunedì Segunda-feira Maandag 月

24

Tuesday Dienstag Mardi Martes Martedì Terça-feira Dinsdag 火

○   (IL) Tu B'Shevat

25

Wednesday Mittwoch Mercredi Miércoles Mercoledì Quarta-feira Woensdag 水

26

Thursday Donnerstag Jeudi Jueves Giovedì Quinta-feira Donderdag 木

27

Friday Freitag Vendredi Viernes Venerdì Sexta-feira Vrijdag 金

28

Saturday Samstag Samedi Sábado Sabato Sábado Zaterdag 土

29

Sunday Sonntag Dimanche Domingo Domenica Domingo Zondag 日

30

5.■ WEEK

01|02.2005

Monday Montag Lundi Lunes Lunedì Segunda-feira Maandag 月

31

Tuesday Dienstag Mardi Martes Martedì Terça-feira Dinsdag 火

1

Wednesday Mittwoch Mercredi Miércoles Mercoledì Quarta-feira Woensdag 水

2

Thursday Donnerstag Jeudi Jueves Giovedì Quinta-feira Donderdag 木

3

Friday Freitag Vendredi Viernes Venerdì Sexta-feira Vrijdag 金

4

Saturday Samstag Samedi Sábado Sabato Sábado Zaterdag 土

5

Sunday Sonntag Dimanche Domingo Domenica Domingo Zondag 日

6

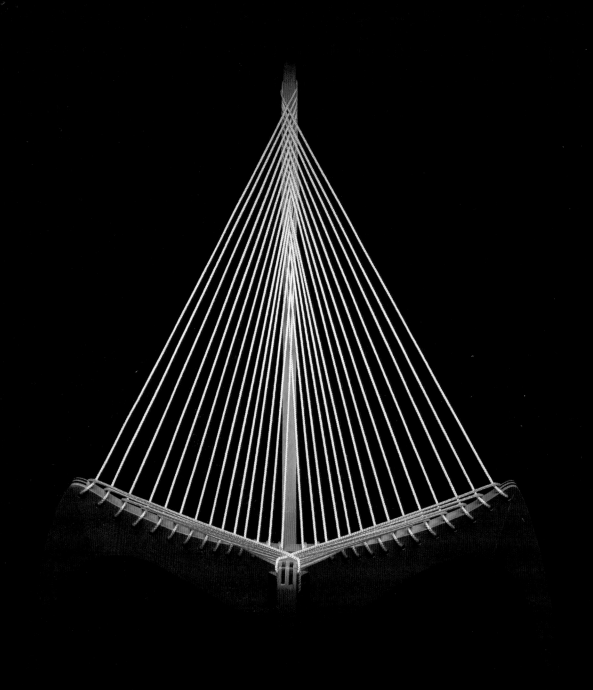

6. WEEK

02.2005

Monday	7	14	21	28	7
Tuesday	8	15	22	1	8
Wednesday	9	16	23	2	9
Thursday	10	17	24	3	10
Friday	11	18	25	4	11
Saturday	12	19	26	5	12
Sunday	13	20	27	6	13
WEEK	**6**	**7**	**8**	**9**	**10**

Monday Montag Lundi Lunes Lunedì Segunda-feira Maandag 月

7

Tuesday Dienstag Mardi Martes Martedì Terça-feira Dinsdag 火

●

8

Wednesday Mittwoch Mercredi Miércoles Mercoledì Quarta-feira Woensdag 水

9

Thursday Donnerstag Jeudi Jueves Giovedì Quinta-feira Donderdag 木

10

Friday Freitag Vendredi Viernes Venerdì Sexta-feira Vrijdag 金

Ⓙ Commemoration of the Founding
of the Nation

11

Saturday Samstag Samedi Sábado Sabato Sábado Zaterdag 土

12

Sunday Sonntag Dimanche Domingo Domenica Domingo Zondag 日

13

7. WEEK

02.2005

Monday	14	21	28	7	14
Tuesday	15	22	1	8	15
Wednesday	16	23	2	9	16
Thursday	17	24	3	10	17
Friday	18	25	4	11	18
Saturday	19	26	5	12	19
Sunday	20	27	6	13	20
WEEK	7	8	9	10	11

Monday Montag Lundi Lunes Lunedì Segunda-feira Maandag 月

14

Tuesday Dienstag Mardi Martes Martedì Terça-feira Dinsdag 火

15

Wednesday Mittwoch Mercredi Miércoles Mercoledì Quarta-feira Woensdag 水

◑

16

Thursday Donnerstag Jeudi Jueves Giovedì Quinta-feira Donderdag 木

17

Friday Freitag Vendredi Viernes Venerdì Sexta-feira Vrijdag 金

18

Saturday Samstag Samedi Sábado Sabato Sábado Zaterdag 土

19

Sunday Sonntag Dimanche Domingo Domenica Domingo Zondag 日

20

8. WEEK

Monday	21	28	7	14	21
Tuesday	22	1	8	15	22
Wednesday	23	2	9	16	23
Thursday	24	3	10	17	24
Friday	25	4	11	18	25
Saturday	26	5	12	19	26
Sunday	27	6	13	20	27
WEEK	**8**	**9**	**10**	**11**	**12**

Monday Montag Lundi Lunes Lunedì Segunda-feira Maandag 月

(USA) President's Day

21

Tuesday Dienstag Mardi Martes Martedì Terça-feira Dinsdag 火

22

Wednesday Mittwoch Mercredi Miércoles Mercoledì Quarta-feira Woensdag 水

23

Thursday Donnerstag Jeudi Jueves Giovedì Quinta-feira Donderdag 木

○

24

Friday Freitag Vendredi Viernes Venerdì Sexta-feira Vrijdag 金

25

Saturday Samstag Samedi Sábado Sabato Sábado Zaterdag 土

26

Sunday Sonntag Dimanche Domingo Domenica Domingo Zondag 日

27

---

9. ∎ WEEK

02|03.2005

Monday Montag Lundi Lunes Lunedì Segunda-feira Maandag 月

28

Tuesday Dienstag Mardi Martes Martedì Terça-feira Dinsdag 火

(ROK) Independence Movement Day

1

Wednesday Mittwoch Mercredi Miércoles Mercoledì Quarta-feira Woensdag 水

2

Thursday Donnerstag Jeudi Jueves Giovedì Quinta-feira Donderdag 木

◑

3

Friday Freitag Vendredi Viernes Venerdì Sexta-feira Vrijdag 金

4

Saturday Samstag Samedi Sábado Sabato Sábado Zaterdag 土

5

Sunday Sonntag Dimanche Domingo Domenica Domingo Zondag 日

6

10. WEEK

03.2005

Monday	7	14	21	28	4
Tuesday	8	15	22	29	5
Wednesday	9	16	23	30	6
Thursday	10	17	24	31	7
Friday	11	18	25	1	8
Saturday	12	19	26	2	9
Sunday	13	20	27	3	10
WEEK	10	11	12	13	14

Monday Montag Lundi Lunes Lunedì Segunda-feira Maandag 月

7

Tuesday Dienstag Mardi Martes Martedì Terça-feira Dinsdag 火

8

Wednesday Mittwoch Mercredi Miércoles Mercoledì Quarta-feira Woensdag 水

9

Thursday Donnerstag Jeudi Jueves Giovedì Quinta-feira Donderdag 木
●

10

Friday Freitag Vendredi Viernes Venerdì Sexta-feira Vrijdag 金

11

Saturday Samstag Samedi Sábado Sabato Sábado Zaterdag 土

12

Sunday Sonntag Dimanche Domingo Domenica Domingo Zondag 日

13

11. WEEK

03.2005

Monday	14	21	28	4	11
Tuesday	15	22	29	5	12
Wednesday	16	23	30	6	13
Thursday	17	24	31	7	14
Friday	18	25	1	8	15
Saturday	19	26	2	9	16
Sunday	20	27	3	10	17
WEEK	**11**	**12**	**13**	**14**	**15**

Monday Montag Lundi Lunes Lunedì Segunda-feira Maandag 月

14

Tuesday Dienstag Mardi Martes Martedì Terça-feira Dinsdag 火

15

Wednesday Mittwoch Mercredi Miércoles Mercoledì Quarta-feira Woensdag 水

16

Thursday Donnerstag Jeudi Jueves Giovedì Quinta-feira Donderdag 木

◗

17

(UK) Saint Patrick's Day
(Northern Ireland only)
(IRL) Saint Patrick's Day

Friday Freitag Vendredi Viernes Venerdì Sexta-feira Vrijdag 金

18

Saturday Samstag Samedi Sábado Sabato Sábado Zaterdag 土

19

Sunday Sonntag Dimanche Domingo Domenica Domingo Zondag 日

(J) Vernal Equinox Day

20

12. WEEK

03.2005

Monday	21	28	4	11	18
Tuesday	22	29	5	12	19
Wednesday	23	30	6	13	20
Thursday	24	31	7	14	21
Friday	25	1	8	15	22
Saturday	26	2	9	16	23
Sunday	27	3	10	17	24
WEEK	**12**	**13**	**14**	**15**	**16**

Monday Montag Lundi Lunes Lunedì Segunda-feira Maandag 月

(J) Public Holiday

21

Tuesday Dienstag Mardi Martes Martedì Terça-feira Dinsdag 火

22

Wednesday Mittwoch Mercredi Miércoles Mercoledì Quarta-feira Woensdag 水

23

Thursday Donnerstag Jeudi Jueves Giovedì Quinta-feira Donderdag 木

24

Friday Freitag Vendredi Viernes Venerdì Sexta-feira Vrijdag 金

○

25

(UK) (CDN) (D) (CH) (E) (P)
Good Friday | Vendredi Saint |
Karfreitag | Venerdì Santo |
Viernes Santo | Sexta-feira Santa
(IL) Purim

Saturday Samstag Samedi Sábado Sabato Sábado Zaterdag 土

26

Sunday Sonntag Dimanche Domingo Domenica Domingo Zondag 日

Easter Sunday | Pâques | Ostersonntag |
Pasqua | 1e Paasdag | Pascua |
Domingo de Páscoa

27

13. WEEK

03|04.2005

Monday	28	4	11	18	25
Tuesday	29	5	12	19	26
Wednesday	30	6	13	20	27
Thursday	31	7	14	21	28
Friday	1	8	15	22	29
Saturday	2	9	16	23	30
Sunday	3	10	17	24	1
WEEK	**13**	**14**	**15**	**16**	**17**

Monday Montag Lundi Lunes Lunedì Segunda-feira Maandag 月

(UK) Easter Monday (except Scotland)
(IRL) (CDN) (F) (D) (A) (CH) (NL) (I)
Easter Monday | Lundi de Pâques |
Ostermontag | Lunedì di Pasqua |
2e Paasdag | Lunedì dell'Angelo

28

Tuesday Dienstag Mardi Martes Martedì Terça-feira Dinsdag 火

29

Wednesday Mittwoch Mercredi Miércoles Mercoledì Quarta-feira Woensdag 水

30

Thursday Donnerstag Jeudi Jueves Giovedì Quinta-feira Donderdag 木

31

Friday Freitag Vendredi Viernes Venerdì Sexta-feira Vrijdag 金

1

Saturday Samstag Samedi Sábado Sabato Sábado Zaterdag 土

◐

2

Sunday Sonntag Dimanche Domingo Domenica Domingo Zondag 日

3

14. WEEK

04.2005

Monday	4	11	18	25	2
Tuesday	5	12	19	26	3
Wednesday	6	13	20	27	4
Thursday	7	14	21	28	5
Friday	8	15	22	29	6
Saturday	9	16	23	30	7
Sunday	10	17	24	1	8
WEEK	**14**	**15**	**16**	**17**	**18**

Monday Montag Lundi Lunes Lunedì Segunda-feira Maandag 月

4

Tuesday Dienstag Mardi Martes Martedì Terça-feira Dinsdag 火

(ROK) Arbor Day

5

Wednesday Mittwoch Mercredi Miércoles Mercoledì Quarta-feira Woensdag 水

6

Thursday Donnerstag Jeudi Jueves Giovedì Quinta-feira Donderdag 木

7

Friday Freitag Vendredi Viernes Venerdì Sexta-feira Vrijdag 金

●

8

Saturday Samstag Samedi Sábado Sabato Sábado Zaterdag 土

9

Sunday Sonntag Dimanche Domingo Domenica Domingo Zondag 日

10

15. WEEK

04.2005

Monday	11	18	25	2	9
Tuesday	12	19	26	3	10
Wednesday	13	20	27	4	11
Thursday	14	21	28	5	12
Friday	15	22	29	6	13
Saturday	16	23	30	7	14
Sunday	17	24	1	8	15
WEEK	15	16	17	18	19

Monday Montag Lundi Lunes Lunedì Segunda-feira Maandag 月

11

Tuesday Dienstag Mardi Martes Martedì Terça-feira Dinsdag 火

12

Wednesday Mittwoch Mercredi Miércoles Mercoledì Quarta-feira Woensdag 水

13

Thursday Donnerstag Jeudi Jueves Giovedì Quinta-feira Donderdag 木

14

Friday Freitag Vendredi Viernes Venerdì Sexta-feira Vrijdag 金

15

Saturday Samstag Samedi Sábado Sabato Sábado Zaterdag 土

◐

16

Sunday Sonntag Dimanche Domingo Domenica Domingo Zondag 日

17

16. WEEK

04.2005

Monday	18	25	2	9	16
Tuesday	19	26	3	10	17
Wednesday	20	27	4	11	18
Thursday	21	28	5	12	19
Friday	22	29	6	13	20
Saturday	23	30	7	14	21
Sunday	24	1	8	15	22
WEEK	**16**	**17**	**18**	**19**	**20**

Monday Montag Lundi Lunes Lunedì Segunda-feira Maandag 月

18

Tuesday Dienstag Mardi Martes Martedì Terça-feira Dinsdag 火

19

Wednesday Mittwoch Mercredi Miércoles Mercoledì Quarta-feira Woensdag 水

20

Thursday Donnerstag Jeudi Jueves Giovedì Quinta-feira Donderdag 木

21

Friday Freitag Vendredi Viernes Venerdì Sexta-feira Vrijdag 金

22

Saturday Samstag Samedi Sábado Sabato Sábado Zaterdag 土

23

Sunday Sonntag Dimanche Domingo Domenica Domingo Zondag 日

○   (IL) Passover

24

17. WEEK

04|05.2005

Monday	25	2	9	16	23
Tuesday	26	3	10	17	24
Wednesday	27	4	11	18	25
Thursday	28	5	12	19	26
Friday	29	6	13	20	27
Saturday	30	7	14	21	28
Sunday	1	8	15	22	29
WEEK	**17**	**18**	**19**	**20**	**21**

Monday Montag Lundi Lunes Lunedì Segunda-feira Maandag 月

(I) Liberazione
(P) Dia da Liberdade

25

Tuesday Dienstag Mardi Martes Martedì Terça-feira Dinsdag 火

26

Wednesday Mittwoch Mercredi Miércoles Mercoledì Quarta-feira Woensdag 水

27

Thursday Donnerstag Jeudi Jueves Giovedì Quinta-feira Donderdag 木

28

Friday Freitag Vendredi Viernes Venerdì Sexta-feira Vrijdag 金

(J) Greenery Day

29

Saturday Samstag Samedi Sábado Sabato Sábado Zaterdag 土

(NL) Koninginnedag

30

Sunday Sonntag Dimanche Domingo Domenica Domingo Zondag 日

(F) (D) (A) (I) (P)
Fête du Travail | Maifeiertag |
Festa del Lavoro | Dia do Trabalhador
(IL) Passover

1

18. WEEK

05.2005

Monday	2	9	16	23	30
Tuesday	3	10	17	24	31
Wednesday	4	11	18	25	1
Thursday	5	12	19	26	2
Friday	6	13	20	27	3
Saturday	7	14	21	28	4
Sunday	8	15	22	29	5
WEEK	18	19	20	21	22

Monday Montag Lundi Lunes Lunedì Segunda-feira Maandag 月

(UK) (IRL)
Early May Bank Holiday
(E) Fiesta del Trabajo

2

Tuesday Dienstag Mardi Martes Martedì Terça-feira Dinsdag 火

(J) Constitution Day

3

Wednesday Mittwoch Mercredi Miércoles Mercoledì Quarta-feira Woensdag 水

(J) Public Holiday

4

Thursday Donnerstag Jeudi Jueves Giovedì Quinta-feira Donderdag 木

(F) (D) (A) (CH) (NL)
Ascension | Christi Himmelfahrt |
Auffahrt | Ascensione | Hemelvaartsdag
(J) (ROK) Children's Day
(IL) Yom Hashoah

5

Friday Freitag Vendredi Viernes Venerdì Sexta-feira Vrijdag 金

6

Saturday Samstag Samedi Sábado Sabato Sábado Zaterdag 土

7

Sunday Sonntag Dimanche Domingo Domenica Domingo Zondag 日

●
(F) Fête de la Libération

8

19. WEEK

05.2005

Monday	9	16	23	30	6
Tuesday	10	17	24	31	7
Wednesday	11	18	25	1	8
Thursday	12	19	26	2	9
Friday	13	20	27	3	10
Saturday	14	21	28	4	11
Sunday	15	22	29	5	12
WEEK	**19**	**20**	**21**	**22**	**23**

Monday Montag Lundi Lunes Lunedì Segunda-feira Maandag 月

9

Tuesday Dienstag Mardi Martes Martedì Terça-feira Dinsdag 火

10

Wednesday Mittwoch Mercredi Miércoles Mercoledì Quarta-feira Woensdag 水

11

Thursday Donnerstag Jeudi Jueves Giovedì Quinta-feira Donderdag 木

(IL) Yom Haazmaut

12

Friday Freitag Vendredi Viernes Venerdì Sexta-feira Vrijdag 金

13

Saturday Samstag Samedi Sábado Sabato Sábado Zaterdag 土

14

Sunday Sonntag Dimanche Domingo Domenica Domingo Zondag 日

(F) (D) (A) (CH) (NL)
Pentecôte | Pfingstsonntag |
Pentecoste | 1e Pinksterdag
(ROK) Buddha's Birthday

15

20.WEEK

05.2005

Monday	16	23	30	6	13
Tuesday	17	24	31	7	14
Wednesday	18	25	1	8	15
Thursday	19	26	2	9	16
Friday	20	27	3	10	17
Saturday	21	28	4	11	18
Sunday	22	29	5	12	19
WEEK	**20**	**21**	**22**	**23**	**24**

Monday Montag Lundi Lunes Lunedì Segunda-feira Maandag 月

◐

Ⓓ Ⓐ Ⓒⓗ Ⓝⓛ
Pfingstmontag | Lundi de Pentecôte |
Lunedì di Pentecoste | 2ᵉ Pinksterdag

16

Tuesday Dienstag Mardi Martes Martedì Terça-feira Dinsdag 火

17

Wednesday Mittwoch Mercredi Miércoles Mercoledì Quarta-feira Woensdag 水

18

Thursday Donnerstag Jeudi Jueves Giovedì Quinta-feira Donderdag 木

19

Friday Freitag Vendredi Viernes Venerdì Sexta-feira Vrijdag 金

20

Saturday Samstag Samedi Sábado Sabato Sábado Zaterdag 土

21

Sunday Sonntag Dimanche Domingo Domenica Domingo Zondag 日

22

21. WEEK

05.2005

Monday	23	30	6	13	20
Tuesday	24	31	7	14	21
Wednesday	25	1	8	15	22
Thursday	26	2	9	16	23
Friday	27	3	10	17	24
Saturday	28	4	11	18	25
Sunday	29	5	12	19	26
WEEK	**21**	**22**	**23**	**24**	**25**

Monday Montag Lundi Lunes Lunedì Segunda-feira Maandag 月

○   ⓒ Victoria Day | Fête de la Reine

23

Tuesday Dienstag Mardi Martes Martedì Terça-feira Dinsdag 火

24

Wednesday Mittwoch Mercredi Miércoles Mercoledì Quarta-feira Woensdag 水

25

Thursday Donnerstag Jeudi Jueves Giovedì Quinta-feira Donderdag 木

                                                                    Ⓓ Fronleichnam (teilweise)
                                                                    Ⓐ Fronleichnam
                                                                    Ⓟ Corpo de Deus

26

Friday Freitag Vendredi Viernes Venerdì Sexta-feira Vrijdag 金

27

Saturday Samstag Samedi Sábado Sabato Sábado Zaterdag 土

28

Sunday Sonntag Dimanche Domingo Domenica Domingo Zondag 日

29

22. WEEK

05|06.2005

Monday Montag Lundi Lunes Lunedì Segunda-feira Maandag 月

◗　　　　　　　　　　　　　　　　　　　　　　　　(USA) Memorial Day
　　　　　　　　　　　　　　　　　　　　　　　　(UK) Spring Bank Holiday

30

Tuesday Dienstag Mardi Martes Martedì Terça-feira Dinsdag 火

31

Wednesday Mittwoch Mercredi Miércoles Mercoledì Quarta-feira Woensdag 水

1

Thursday Donnerstag Jeudi Jueves Giovedì Quinta-feira Donderdag 木

　　　　　　　　　　　　　　　　　　　　　　　　(I) Festa della Repubblica

2

Friday Freitag Vendredi Viernes Venerdì Sexta-feira Vrijdag 金

3

Saturday Samstag Samedi Sábado Sabato Sábado Zaterdag 土

4

Sunday Sonntag Dimanche Domingo Domenica Domingo Zondag 日

5

23. WEEK

06.2005

Monday	6	13	20	27	4
Tuesday	7	14	21	28	5
Wednesday	8	15	22	29	6
Thursday	9	16	23	30	7
Friday	10	17	24	1	8
Saturday	11	18	25	2	9
Sunday	12	19	26	3	10
WEEK	**23**	**24**	**25**	**26**	**27**

Monday Montag Lundi Lunes Lunedì Segunda-feira Maandag 月

●

(IRL) First Monday in June
(ROK) Memorial Day

6

Tuesday Dienstag Mardi Martes Martedì Terça-feira Dinsdag 火

7

Wednesday Mittwoch Mercredi Miércoles Mercoledì Quarta-feira Woensdag 水

8

Thursday Donnerstag Jeudi Jueves Giovedì Quinta-feira Donderdag 木

9

Friday Freitag Vendredi Viernes Venerdì Sexta-feira Vrijdag 金

(P) Dia Nacional

10

Saturday Samstag Samedi Sábado Sabato Sábado Zaterdag 土

11

Sunday Sonntag Dimanche Domingo Domenica Domingo Zondag 日

12

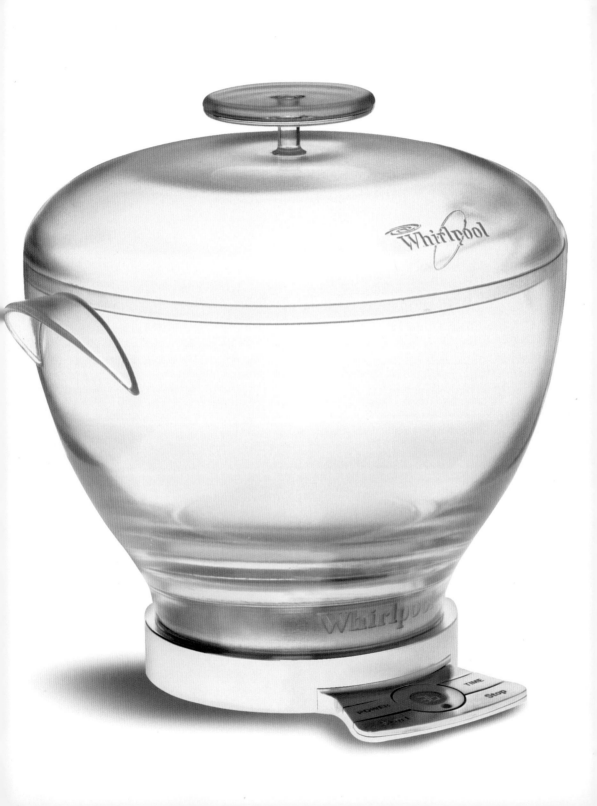

24. WEEK

06.2005

Monday	13	20	27	4	11
Tuesday	14	21	28	5	12
Wednesday	15	22	29	6	13
Thursday	16	23	30	7	14
Friday	17	24	1	8	15
Saturday	18	25	2	9	16
Sunday	19	26	3	10	17
WEEK	**24**	**25**	**26**	**27**	**28**

Monday Montag Lundi Lunes Lunedì Segunda-feira Maandag 月

(IL) Shavuot

13

Tuesday Dienstag Mardi Martes Martedì Terça-feira Dinsdag 火

14

Wednesday Mittwoch Mercredi Miércoles Mercoledì Quarta-feira Woensdag 水

◖

15

Thursday Donnerstag Jeudi Jueves Giovedì Quinta-feira Donderdag 木

16

Friday Freitag Vendredi Viernes Venerdì Sexta-feira Vrijdag 金

17

Saturday Samstag Samedi Sábado Sabato Sábado Zaterdag 土

18

Sunday Sonntag Dimanche Domingo Domenica Domingo Zondag 日

19

25.■ WEEK

06.2005

Monday	20	27	4	11	18
Tuesday	21	28	5	12	19
Wednesday	22	29	6	13	20
Thursday	23	30	7	14	21
Friday	24	1	8	15	22
Saturday	25	2	9	16	23
Sunday	26	3	10	17	24
WEEK	25	26	27	28	29

Monday Montag Lundi Lunes Lunedì Segunda-feira Maandag 月

20

Tuesday Dienstag Mardi Martes Martedì Terça-feira Dinsdag 火

21

Wednesday Mittwoch Mercredi Miércoles Mercoledì Quarta-feira Woensdag 水

○

22

Thursday Donnerstag Jeudi Jueves Giovedì Quinta-feira Donderdag 木

23

Friday Freitag Vendredi Viernes Venerdì Sexta-feira Vrijdag 金

24

Saturday Samstag Samedi Sábado Sabato Sábado Zaterdag 土

25

Sunday Sonntag Dimanche Domingo Domenica Domingo Zondag 日

26

26.■ WEEK

06 | 07.2005

Monday	27	4	11	18	25
Tuesday	28	5	12	19	26
Wednesday	29	6	13	20	27
Thursday	30	7	14	21	28
Friday	1	8	15	22	29
Saturday	2	9	16	23	30
Sunday	3	10	17	24	31
WEEK	26	27	28	29	30

Monday Montag Lundi Lunes Lunedì Segunda-feira Maandag 月

27

Tuesday Dienstag Mardi Martes Martedì Terça-feira Dinsdag 火

◐

28

Wednesday Mittwoch Mercredi Miércoles Mercoledì Quarta-feira Woensdag 水

29

Thursday Donnerstag Jeudi Jueves Giovedì Quinta-feira Donderdag 木

30

Friday Freitag Vendredi Viernes Venerdì Sexta-feira Vrijdag 金

(CDN) Canada Day | Fête du Canada

1

Saturday Samstag Samedi Sábado Sabato Sábado Zaterdag 土

2

Sunday Sonntag Dimanche Domingo Domenica Domingo Zondag 日

3

27.∎ WEEK

07.2005

Monday	4	11	18	25	1
Tuesday	5	12	19	26	2
Wednesday	6	13	20	27	3
Thursday	7	14	21	28	4
Friday	8	15	22	29	5
Saturday	9	16	23	30	6
Sunday	10	17	24	31	7
WEEK	**27**	**28**	**29**	**30**	**31**

Monday Montag Lundi Lunes Lunedì Segunda-feira Maandag 月

(USA) Independence Day

4

Tuesday Dienstag Mardi Martes Martedì Terça-feira Dinsdag 火

5

Wednesday Mittwoch Mercredi Miércoles Mercoledì Quarta-feira Woensdag 水

●

6

Thursday Donnerstag Jeudi Jueves Giovedì Quinta-feira Donderdag 木

7

Friday Freitag Vendredi Viernes Venerdì Sexta-feira Vrijdag 金

8

Saturday Samstag Samedi Sábado Sabato Sábado Zaterdag 土

9

Sunday Sonntag Dimanche Domingo Domenica Domingo Zondag 日

10

28. ■ WEEK

07.2005

Monday	11	18	25	1	8
Tuesday	12	19	26	2	9
Wednesday	13	20	27	3	10
Thursday	14	21	28	4	11
Friday	15	22	29	5	12
Saturday	16	23	30	6	13
Sunday	17	24	31	7	14
WEEK	28	29	30	31	32

Monday Montag Lundi Lunes Lunedì Segunda-feira Maandag 月

11

Tuesday Dienstag Mardi Martes Martedì Terça-feira Dinsdag 火

(UK) Battle of the Boyne Day
(Northern Ireland only)

12

Wednesday Mittwoch Mercredi Miércoles Mercoledì Quarta-feira Woensdag 水

13

Thursday Donnerstag Jeudi Jueves Giovedì Quinta-feira Donderdag 木

(F) Fête Nationale

14

Friday Freitag Vendredi Viernes Venerdì Sexta-feira Vrijdag 金

15

Saturday Samstag Samedi Sábado Sabato Sábado Zaterdag 土

16

Sunday Sonntag Dimanche Domingo Domenica Domingo Zondag 日

(ROK) Constitution Day

17

29. ■ WEEK

07.2005

Monday	18	25	1	8	15
Tuesday	19	26	2	9	16
Wednesday	20	27	3	10	17
Thursday	21	28	4	11	18
Friday	22	29	5	12	19
Saturday	23	30	6	13	20
Sunday	24	31	7	14	21
WEEK	29	30	31	32	33

Monday Montag Lundi Lunes Lunedì Segunda-feira Maandag 月

ⓙ Marine Day

18

Tuesday Dienstag Mardi Martes Martedì Terça-feira Dinsdag 火

19

Wednesday Mittwoch Mercredi Miércoles Mercoledì Quarta-feira Woensdag 水

20

Thursday Donnerstag Jeudi Jueves Giovedì Quinta-feira Donderdag 木
○

21

Friday Freitag Vendredi Viernes Venerdì Sexta-feira Vrijdag 金

22

Saturday Samstag Samedi Sábado Sabato Sábado Zaterdag 土

23

Sunday Sonntag Dimanche Domingo Domenica Domingo Zondag 日

24

30. WEEK

07.2005

Monday	25	1	8	15	22
Tuesday	26	2	9	16	23
Wednesday	27	3	10	17	24
Thursday	28	4	11	18	25
Friday	29	5	12	19	26
Saturday	30	6	13	20	27
Sunday	31	7	14	21	28
WEEK	**30**	**31**	**32**	**33**	**34**

Monday Montag Lundi Lunes Lunedì Segunda-feira Maandag 月

25

Tuesday Dienstag Mardi Martes Martedì Terça-feira Dinsdag 火

26

Wednesday Mittwoch Mercredi Miércoles Mercoledì Quarta-feira Woensdag 水

27

Thursday Donnerstag Jeudi Jueves Giovedì Quinta-feira Donderdag 木

◑

28

Friday Freitag Vendredi Viernes Venerdì Sexta-feira Vrijdag 金

29

Saturday Samstag Samedi Sábado Sabato Sábado Zaterdag 土

30

Sunday Sonntag Dimanche Domingo Domenica Domingo Zondag 日

31

31. ■ WEEK

08.2005

Monday Montag Lundi Lunes Lunedì Segunda-feira Maandag 月

(UK) Summer Bank Holiday
(Scotland only)
(IRL) First Monday in August
(CH) Bundesfeiertag | Fête nationale |
Festa nazionale

1

Tuesday Dienstag Mardi Martes Martedì Terça-feira Dinsdag 火

2

Wednesday Mittwoch Mercredi Miércoles Mercoledì Quarta-feira Woensdag 水

3

Thursday Donnerstag Jeudi Jueves Giovedì Quinta-feira Donderdag 木

4

Friday Freitag Vendredi Viernes Venerdì Sexta-feira Vrijdag 金

●

5

Saturday Samstag Samedi Sábado Sabato Sábado Zaterdag 土

6

Sunday Sonntag Dimanche Domingo Domenica Domingo Zondag 日

7

UP IN THE TREE

DOWN ON THE GROUND

32. WEEK

08.2005

Monday	8	15	22	29	5
Tuesday	9	16	23	30	6
Wednesday	10	17	24	31	7
Thursday	11	18	25	1	8
Friday	12	19	26	2	9
Saturday	13	20	27	3	10
Sunday	14	21	28	4	11
WEEK	**32**	**33**	**34**	**35**	**36**

Monday Montag Lundi Lunes Lunedì Segunda-feira Maandag 月

8

Tuesday Dienstag Mardi Martes Martedì Terça-feira Dinsdag 火

9

Wednesday Mittwoch Mercredi Miércoles Mercoledì Quarta-feira Woensdag 水

10

Thursday Donnerstag Jeudi Jueves Giovedì Quinta-feira Donderdag 木

11

Friday Freitag Vendredi Viernes Venerdì Sexta-feira Vrijdag 金

12

Saturday Samstag Samedi Sábado Sabato Sábado Zaterdag 土

13

Sunday Sonntag Dimanche Domingo Domenica Domingo Zondag 日

(IL) Tisha B'Av

14

33. ■ WEEK

08.2005

Monday Montag Lundi Lunes Lunedì Segunda-feira Maandag 月

15

Ⓓ Mariä Himmelfahrt (teilweise)

Ⓕ Ⓐ Ⓔ Ⓘ Ⓟ

Assomption | Mariä Himmelfahrt |

Asunción de la Virgen | Assunzione |

Assunção de Nossa Senhora

ⓇⓄⓀ Independence Day

Tuesday Dienstag Mardi Martes Martedì Terça-feira Dinsdag 火

16

Wednesday Mittwoch Mercredi Miércoles Mercoledì Quarta-feira Woensdag 水

17

Thursday Donnerstag Jeudi Jueves Giovedì Quinta-feira Donderdag 木

18

Friday Freitag Vendredi Viernes Venerdì Sexta-feira Vrijdag 金

○

19

Saturday Samstag Samedi Sábado Sabato Sábado Zaterdag 土

20

Sunday Sonntag Dimanche Domingo Domenica Domingo Zondag 日

21

34. WEEK

08.2005

Monday	22	29	5	12	19
Tuesday	23	30	6	13	20
Wednesday	24	31	7	14	21
Thursday	25	1	8	15	22
Friday	26	2	9	16	23
Saturday	27	3	10	17	24
Sunday	28	4	11	18	25
WEEK	**34**	**35**	**36**	**37**	**38**

Monday Montag Lundi Lunes Lunedì Segunda-feira Maandag 月

22

Tuesday Dienstag Mardi Martes Martedì Terça-feira Dinsdag 火

23

Wednesday Mittwoch Mercredi Miércoles Mercoledì Quarta-feira Woensdag 水

24

Thursday Donnerstag Jeudi Jueves Giovedì Quinta-feira Donderdag 木

25

Friday Freitag Vendredi Viernes Venerdì Sexta-feira Vrijdag 金

26

Saturday Samstag Samedi Sábado Sabato Sábado Zaterdag 土

27

Sunday Sonntag Dimanche Domingo Domenica Domingo Zondag 日

28

35. WEEK

08|09.2005

Monday	29	5	12	19	26
Tuesday	30	6	13	20	27
Wednesday	31	7	14	21	28
Thursday	1	8	15	22	29
Friday	2	9	16	23	30
Saturday	3	10	17	24	1
Sunday	4	11	18	25	2
WEEK	35	36	37	38	39

Monday Montag Lundi Lunes Lunedì Segunda-feira Maandag 月

(UK) Summer Bank Holiday
(except Scotland)

29

Tuesday Dienstag Mardi Martes Martedì Terça-feira Dinsdag 火

30

Wednesday Mittwoch Mercredi Miércoles Mercoledì Quarta-feira Woensdag 水

31

Thursday Donnerstag Jeudi Jueves Giovedì Quinta-feira Donderdag 木

1

Friday Freitag Vendredi Viernes Venerdì Sexta-feira Vrijdag 金

2

Saturday Samstag Samedi Sábado Sabato Sábado Zaterdag 土

• 3

Sunday Sonntag Dimanche Domingo Domenica Domingo Zondag 日

4

36. WEEK

09.2005

Monday	5	12	19	26	3
Tuesday	6	13	20	27	4
Wednesday	7	14	21	28	5
Thursday	8	15	22	29	6
Friday	9	16	23	30	7
Saturday	10	17	24	1	8
Sunday	11	18	25	2	9
WEEK	**36**	**37**	**38**	**39**	**40**

Monday Montag Lundi Lunes Lunedì Segunda-feira Maandag 月

(USA) Labor Day
(CDN) Labour Day | Fête du Travail

5

Tuesday Dienstag Mardi Martes Martedì Terça-feira Dinsdag 火

6

Wednesday Mittwoch Mercredi Miércoles Mercoledì Quarta-feira Woensdag 水

7

Thursday Donnerstag Jeudi Jueves Giovedì Quinta-feira Donderdag 木

8

Friday Freitag Vendredi Viernes Venerdì Sexta-feira Vrijdag 金

9

Saturday Samstag Samedi Sábado Sabato Sábado Zaterdag 土

10

Sunday Sonntag Dimanche Domingo Domenica Domingo Zondag 日

11

37. WEEK

09.2005

Monday	12	19	26	3	10
Tuesday	13	20	27	4	11
Wednesday	14	21	28	5	12
Thursday	15	22	29	6	13
Friday	16	23	30	7	14
Saturday	17	24	1	8	15
Sunday	18	25	2	9	16
WEEK	**37**	**38**	**39**	**40**	**41**

Monday Montag Lundi Lunes Lunedì Segunda-feira Maandag 月

12

Tuesday Dienstag Mardi Martes Martedì Terça-feira Dinsdag 火

13

Wednesday Mittwoch Mercredi Miércoles Mercoledì Quarta-feira Woensdag 水

14

Thursday Donnerstag Jeudi Jueves Giovedì Quinta-feira Donderdag 木

15

Friday Freitag Vendredi Viernes Venerdì Sexta-feira Vrijdag 金

16

Saturday Samstag Samedi Sábado Sabato Sábado Zaterdag 土

17

Sunday Sonntag Dimanche Domingo Domenica Domingo Zondag 日

○   (ROK) Chuseok

18

38. ■ WEEK

09.2005

Monday Montag Lundi Lunes Lunedì Segunda-feira Maandag 月

Ⓙ Respect-for-the-Aged Day

19

Tuesday Dienstag Mardi Martes Martedì Terça-feira Dinsdag 火

20

Wednesday Mittwoch Mercredi Miércoles Mercoledì Quarta-feira Woensdag 水

21

Thursday Donnerstag Jeudi Jueves Giovedì Quinta-feira Donderdag 木

22

Friday Freitag Vendredi Viernes Venerdì Sexta-feira Vrijdag 金

Ⓙ Autumn Equinox Day

23

Saturday Samstag Samedi Sábado Sabato Sábado Zaterdag 土

24

Sunday Sonntag Dimanche Domingo Domenica Domingo Zondag 日

◗

25

39. ■ WEEK

09|10.2005

Monday	26	3	10	17	24
Tuesday	27	4	11	18	25
Wednesday	28	5	12	19	26
Thursday	29	6	13	20	27
Friday	30	7	14	21	28
Saturday	1	8	15	22	29
Sunday	2	9	16	23	30
WEEK	**39**	**40**	**41**	**42**	**43**

Monday Montag Lundi Lunes Lunedì Segunda-feira Maandag 月

26

Tuesday Dienstag Mardi Martes Martedì Terça-feira Dinsdag 火

27

Wednesday Mittwoch Mercredi Miércoles Mercoledì Quarta-feira Woensdag 水

28

Thursday Donnerstag Jeudi Jueves Giovedì Quinta-feira Donderdag 木

29

Friday Freitag Vendredi Viernes Venerdì Sexta-feira Vrijdag 金

30

Saturday Samstag Samedi Sábado Sabato Sábado Zaterdag 土

1

Sunday Sonntag Dimanche Domingo Domenica Domingo Zondag 日

2

40. WEEK

10.2005

Monday	3	10	17	24	31
Tuesday	4	11	18	25	1
Wednesday	5	12	19	26	2
Thursday	6	13	20	27	3
Friday	7	14	21	28	4
Saturday	8	15	22	29	5
Sunday	9	16	23	30	6
WEEK	**40**	**41**	**42**	**43**	**44**

Monday Montag Lundi Lunes Lunedì Segunda-feira Maandag 月

●

Ⓓ Tag der Deutschen Einheit
ⓇⓄⓀ National Foundation Day

3

Tuesday Dienstag Mardi Martes Martedì Terça-feira Dinsdag 火

Ⓘⓛ Rosh Hashanah

4

Wednesday Mittwoch Mercredi Miércoles Mercoledì Quarta-feira Woensdag 水

Ⓟ Implantação da República
Ⓘⓛ Rosh Hashanah

5

Thursday Donnerstag Jeudi Jueves Giovedì Quinta-feira Donderdag 木

6

Friday Freitag Vendredi Viernes Venerdì Sexta-feira Vrijdag 金

7

Saturday Samstag Samedi Sábado Sabato Sábado Zaterdag 土

8

Sunday Sonntag Dimanche Domingo Domenica Domingo Zondag 日

9

41. WEEK

10.2005

Monday	10	17	24	31	7
Tuesday	11	18	25	1	8
Wednesday	12	19	26	2	9
Thursday	13	20	27	3	10
Friday	14	21	28	4	11
Saturday	15	22	29	5	12
Sunday	16	23	30	6	13
WEEK	**41**	**42**	**43**	**44**	**45**

Monday Montag Lundi Lunes Lunedì Segunda-feira Maandag 月

10

(USA) Columbus Day
(CDN) Thanksgiving Day | Action de Grâces
(J) Health-Sports Day

Tuesday Dienstag Mardi Martes Martedì Terça-feira Dinsdag 火

11

Wednesday Mittwoch Mercredi Miércoles Mercoledì Quarta-feira Woensdag 水

(E) Fiesta Nacional

12

Thursday Donnerstag Jeudi Jueves Giovedì Quinta-feira Donderdag 木

(IL) Yom Kippur

13

Friday Freitag Vendredi Viernes Venerdì Sexta-feira Vrijdag 金

14

Saturday Samstag Samedi Sábado Sabato Sábado Zaterdag 土

15

Sunday Sonntag Dimanche Domingo Domenica Domingo Zondag 日

16

42. WEEK

10.2005

Monday	17	24	31	7	14
Tuesday	18	25	1	8	15
Wednesday	19	26	2	9	16
Thursday	20	27	3	10	17
Friday	21	28	4	11	18
Saturday	22	29	5	12	19
Sunday	23	30	6	13	20
WEEK	42	43	44	45	46

Monday Montag Lundi Lunes Lunedì Segunda-feira Maandag 月

○

17

Tuesday Dienstag Mardi Martes Martedì Terça-feira Dinsdag 火

(IL) Succoth

18

Wednesday Mittwoch Mercredi Miércoles Mercoledì Quarta-feira Woensdag 水

19

Thursday Donnerstag Jeudi Jueves Giovedì Quinta-feira Donderdag 木

20

Friday Freitag Vendredi Viernes Venerdì Sexta-feira Vrijdag 金

21

Saturday Samstag Samedi Sábado Sabato Sábado Zaterdag 土

22

Sunday Sonntag Dimanche Domingo Domenica Domingo Zondag 日

23

43. WEEK

10.2005

Monday Montag Lundi Lunes Lunedì Segunda-feira Maandag 月

24

Tuesday Dienstag Mardi Martes Martedì Terça-feira Dinsdag 火

◗   ⒤ Sh'mini Atzereth

25

Wednesday Mittwoch Mercredi Miércoles Mercoledì Quarta-feira Woensdag 水

Ⓐ Nationalfeiertag
⒤ Simchat Torah

26

Thursday Donnerstag Jeudi Jueves Giovedì Quinta-feira Donderdag 木

27

Friday Freitag Vendredi Viernes Venerdì Sexta-feira Vrijdag 金

28

Saturday Samstag Samedi Sábado Sabato Sábado Zaterdag 土

29

Sunday Sonntag Dimanche Domingo Domenica Domingo Zondag 日

30

44. WEEK

10 | 11.2005

Monday	31	7	14	21	28
Tuesday	1	8	15	22	29
Wednesday	2	9	16	23	30
Thursday	3	10	17	24	1
Friday	4	11	18	25	2
Saturday	5	12	19	26	3
Sunday	6	13	20	27	4
WEEK	**44**	**45**	**46**	**47**	**48**

Monday Montag Lundi Lunes Lunedì Segunda-feira Maandag 月

(IRL) Last Monday in October

(D) Reformationstag (teilweise)

31

Tuesday Dienstag Mardi Martes Martedì Terça-feira Dinsdag 火

(D) Allerheiligen (teilweise)

(F) (A) (E) (I) (P)

Toussaint | Allerheiligen | Todos los Santos | Ognissanti | Todos os Santos

1

Wednesday Mittwoch Mercredi Miércoles Mercoledì Quarta-feira Woensdag 水

●

2

Thursday Donnerstag Jeudi Jueves Giovedì Quinta-feira Donderdag 木

(J) Culture Day

3

Friday Freitag Vendredi Viernes Venerdì Sexta-feira Vrijdag 金

4

Saturday Samstag Samedi Sábado Sabato Sábado Zaterdag 土

5

Sunday Sonntag Dimanche Domingo Domenica Domingo Zondag 日

6

---

45. WEEK

11.2005

Monday	7	14	21	28	5
Tuesday	8	15	22	29	6
Wednesday	9	16	23	30	7
Thursday	10	17	24	1	8
Friday	11	18	25	2	9
Saturday	12	19	26	3	10
Sunday	13	20	27	4	11
WEEK	**45**	**46**	**47**	**48**	**49**

Monday Montag Lundi Lunes Lunedì Segunda-feira Maandag 月

7

Tuesday Dienstag Mardi Martes Martedì Terça-feira Dinsdag 火

8

Wednesday Mittwoch Mercredi Miércoles Mercoledì Quarta-feira Woensdag 水

◐

9

Thursday Donnerstag Jeudi Jueves Giovedì Quinta-feira Donderdag 木

10

Friday Freitag Vendredi Viernes Venerdì Sexta-feira Vrijdag 金

11

(USA) Veterans' Day
(CDN) Remembrance Day | Jour du Souvenir
(F) Armistice 1918

Saturday Samstag Samedi Sábado Sabato Sábado Zaterdag 土

12

Sunday Sonntag Dimanche Domingo Domenica Domingo Zondag 日

13

46. WEEK

11.2005

Monday	14	21	28	5	12
Tuesday	15	22	29	6	13
Wednesday	16	23	30	7	14
Thursday	17	24	1	8	15
Friday	18	25	2	9	16
Saturday	19	26	3	10	17
Sunday	20	27	4	11	18
WEEK	**46**	**47**	**48**	**49**	**50**

Monday Montag Lundi Lunes Lunedì Segunda-feira Maandag 月

14

Tuesday Dienstag Mardi Martes Martedì Terça-feira Dinsdag 火

15

Wednesday Mittwoch Mercredi Miércoles Mercoledì Quarta-feira Woensdag 水

○   ⒟ Buß- und Bettag (teilweise)

16

Thursday Donnerstag Jeudi Jueves Giovedì Quinta-feira Donderdag 木

17

Friday Freitag Vendredi Viernes Venerdì Sexta-feira Vrijdag 金

18

Saturday Samstag Samedi Sábado Sabato Sábado Zaterdag 土

19

Sunday Sonntag Dimanche Domingo Domenica Domingo Zondag 日

20

47. WEEK

11.2005

Monday	21	28	5	12	19
Tuesday	22	29	6	13	20
Wednesday	23	30	7	14	21
Thursday	24	1	8	15	22
Friday	25	2	9	16	23
Saturday	26	3	10	17	24
Sunday	27	4	11	18	25
WEEK	**47**	**48**	**49**	**50**	**51**

Monday Montag Lundi Lunes Lunedì Segunda-feira Maandag 月

21

Tuesday Dienstag Mardi Martes Martedì Terça-feira Dinsdag 火

22

Wednesday Mittwoch Mercredi Miércoles Mercoledì Quarta-feira Woensdag 水

◑   (J) Labor-Thanksgiving Day

23

Thursday Donnerstag Jeudi Jueves Giovedì Quinta-feira Donderdag 木

(USA) Thanksgiving Day

24

Friday Freitag Vendredi Viernes Venerdì Sexta-feira Vrijdag 金

25

Saturday Samstag Samedi Sábado Sabato Sábado Zaterdag 土

26

Sunday Sonntag Dimanche Domingo Domenica Domingo Zondag 日

27

48. WEEK

11|12.2005

Monday	28	5	12	19	26
Tuesday	29	6	13	20	27
Wednesday	30	7	14	21	28
Thursday	1	8	15	22	29
Friday	2	9	16	23	30
Saturday	3	10	17	24	31
Sunday	4	11	18	25	1
WEEK	**48**	**49**	**50**	**51**	**52**

Monday Montag Lundi Lunes Lunedì Segunda-feira Maandag 月

28

Tuesday Dienstag Mardi Martes Martedì Terça-feira Dinsdag 火

29

Wednesday Mittwoch Mercredi Miércoles Mercoledì Quarta-feira Woensdag 水

30

Thursday Donnerstag Jeudi Jueves Giovedì Quinta-feira Donderdag 木

●   Ⓟ Dia da Restauração

1

Friday Freitag Vendredi Viernes Venerdì Sexta-feira Vrijdag 金

2

Saturday Samstag Samedi Sábado Sabato Sábado Zaterdag 土

3

Sunday Sonntag Dimanche Domingo Domenica Domingo Zondag 日

4

49. ■ WEEK

12.2005

Monday	5	12	19	26	2
Tuesday	6	13	20	27	3
Wednesday	7	14	21	28	4
Thursday	8	15	22	29	5
Friday	9	16	23	30	6
Saturday	10	17	24	31	7
Sunday	11	18	25	1	8
WEEK	49	50	51	52	1

Monday Montag Lundi Lunes Lunedì Segunda-feira Maandag 月

5

Tuesday Dienstag Mardi Martes Martedì Terça-feira Dinsdag 火

Ⓔ Día de la Constitución

6

Wednesday Mittwoch Mercredi Miércoles Mercoledì Quarta-feira Woensdag 水

7

Thursday Donnerstag Jeudi Jueves Giovedì Quinta-feira Donderdag 木

◗

Ⓐ Ⓔ Ⓘ Ⓟ
Mariä Empfängnis | Inmaculada
Concepción | Immacolata Concezione |
Imaculada Conceição

8

Friday Freitag Vendredi Viernes Venerdì Sexta-feira Vrijdag 金

9

Saturday Samstag Samedi Sábado Sabato Sábado Zaterdag 土

10

Sunday Sonntag Dimanche Domingo Domenica Domingo Zondag 日

11

50. WEEK

12.2005

Monday Montag Lundi Lunes Lunedì Segunda-feira Maandag 月

12

Tuesday Dienstag Mardi Martes Martedì Terça-feira Dinsdag 火

13

Wednesday Mittwoch Mercredi Miércoles Mercoledì Quarta-feira Woensdag 水

14

Thursday Donnerstag Jeudi Jueves Giovedì Quinta-feira Donderdag 木
○

15

Friday Freitag Vendredi Viernes Venerdì Sexta-feira Vrijdag 金

16

Saturday Samstag Samedi Sábado Sabato Sábado Zaterdag 土

17

Sunday Sonntag Dimanche Domingo Domenica Domingo Zondag 日

18

51. ■ WEEK

12.2005

Monday	19	26	2	9	16
Tuesday	20	27	3	10	17
Wednesday	21	28	4	11	18
Thursday	22	29	5	12	19
Friday	23	30	6	13	20
Saturday	24	31	7	14	21
Sunday	25	1	8	15	22
WEEK	51	52	1	2	3

Monday Montag Lundi Lunes Lunedì Segunda-feira Maandag 月

19

Tuesday Dienstag Mardi Martes Martedì Terça-feira Dinsdag 火

20

Wednesday Mittwoch Mercredi Miércoles Mercoledì Quarta-feira Woensdag 水

21

Thursday Donnerstag Jeudi Jueves Giovedì Quinta-feira Donderdag 木

22

Friday Freitag Vendredi Viernes Venerdì Sexta-feira Vrijdag 金

◐   (J) Emperor's Birthday

23

Saturday Samstag Samedi Sábado Sabato Sábado Zaterdag 土

24

Sunday Sonntag Dimanche Domingo Domenica Domingo Zondag 日

(USA) (UK) (IRL) (ROK) (CDN) (F) (D) (A) (CH)
(NL) (E) (I) (P)
Christmas Day | Noël | 1. Weihnachtstag |
Weihnachten | 1e Kerstdag | Natividad
del Señor | Natale | Dia de Natal

25

52. WEEK

12.2005 | 01.2006

Monday	26	2	9	16	23
Tuesday	27	3	10	17	24
Wednesday	28	4	11	18	25
Thursday	29	5	12	19	26
Friday	30	6	13	20	27
Saturday	31	7	14	21	28
Sunday	1	8	15	22	29
WEEK	**52**	**1**	**2**	**3**	**4**

Monday Montag Lundi Lunes Lunedì Segunda-feira Maandag 月

(UK) (IRL) (CDN) (D) (A) (CH) (NL) (I)
Boxing Day | Saint Stephen's Day |
Lendemain de Noël | 2. Weihnachtstag |
Stefanstag | S. Etienne | 2e Kerstdag |
S. Stefano
(IL) Hanukkah

26

Tuesday Dienstag Mardi Martes Martedì Terça-feira Dinsdag 火

(UK) Public Holiday

27

Wednesday Mittwoch Mercredi Miércoles Mercoledì Quarta-feira Woensdag 水

28

Thursday Donnerstag Jeudi Jueves Giovedì Quinta-feira Donderdag 木

29

Friday Freitag Vendredi Viernes Venerdì Sexta-feira Vrijdag 金

30

Saturday Samstag Samedi Sábado Sabato Sábado Zaterdag 土

●

31

Sunday Sonntag Dimanche Domingo Domenica Domingo Zondag 日

New Year's Day | Jour de l'An | Neujahr |
Nieuwjaarsdag | Nieuwjaar | Nouvel An |
Capodanno

1

PUBLIC HOLIDAYS 2005

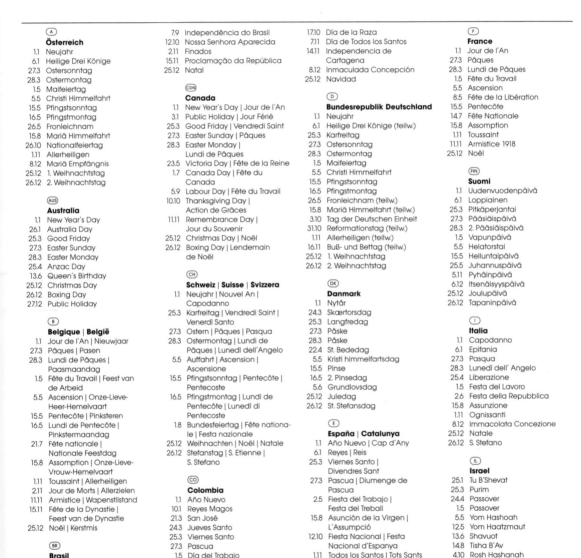

PUBLIC HOLIDAYS 2005

(IRL) Ireland
1.1	New Year's Day
17.3	Saint Patrick's Day
27.3	Easter Sunday
28.3	Easter Monday
2.5	First Monday in May
6.6	First Monday in June
1.8	First Monday in August
31.10	Last Monday in October
25.12	Christmas Day
26.12	Saint Stephen's Day

(J) Japan
1.1	New Year's Day
10.1	Coming-of-Age Day
11.2	Commemoration of the Founding of the Nation
20.3	Vernal Equinox Day
21.3	Public Holiday
29.4	Greenery Day
3.5	Constitution Day
4.5	Public Holiday
5.5	Children's Day
18.7	Marine Day
19.9	Respect-for-the-Aged Day
23.9	Autumn Equinox Day
10.10	Health-Sports Day
3.11	Culture Day
23.11	Labor-Thanksgiving Day
23.12	Emperor's Birthday

(L) Luxembourg
1.1	Jour de l'An
27.3	Pâques
28.3	Lundi de Pâques
1.5	Fête du Travail
5.5	Ascension
15.5	Pentecôte
16.5	Lundi de Pentecôte
23.6	Fête Nationale
15.8	Assomption
1.11	Toussaint
25.12	Noël
26.12	Lendemain de Noël

(MEX) México
1.1	Año Nuevo
5.2	Aniversario de la Constitución
21.3	Natalicio de Benito Juárez
24.3	Jueves Santo
25.3	Viernes Santo
27.3	Pascua
1.5	Día del Trabajo
1.9	Informe presidencial
16.9	Día de la Independencia
20.11	Aniversario de la Revolución Mexicana
25.12	Navidad

(N) Norge
1.1	Nyttårsdag
20.3	Palmesøndag
24.3	Skjærtorsdag
25.3	Langfredag
27.3	1. påskedag
28.3	2. påskedag
1.5	Offentlig høytidsdag
17.5	Grunnlovsdag
5.5	Kristi himmelfartsdag
15.5	1. pinsedag
16.5	2. pinsedag
25.12	1. juledag
26.12	2. juledag

(NL) Nederland
1.1	Nieuwjaarsdag
27.3	1e Paasdag
28.3	2e Paasdag
30.4	Koninginnedag
5.5	Hemelvaartsdag
15.5	1e Pinksterdag
16.5	2e Pinksterdag
25.12	1e Kerstdag
26.12	2e Kerstdag

(NZ) New Zealand
1.1	New Year's Day
2.1	Day after New Year's Day
6.2	Waitangi Day
25.3	Good Friday
27.3	Easter Sunday
28.3	Easter Monday
25.4	Anzac Day
6.6	Queen's Birthday
24.10	Labour Day
25.12	Christmas Day
26.12	Boxing Day
27.12	Public Holiday

(P) Portugal
1.1	Ano Novo
25.3	Sexta-feira Santa
27.3	Domingo de Páscoa
25.4	Dia da Liberdade
1.5	Dia do Trabalhador
26.5	Corpo de Deus
10.6	Dia Nacional
15.8	Assunção de Nossa Senhora
5.10	Implantação da República
1.11	Todos os Santos
1.12	Dia da Restauração
8.12	Imaculada Conceição
25.12	Dia de Natal

(RA) Argentina
1.1	Año Nuevo
24.3	Jueves Santo
25.3	Viernes Santo
27.3	Pascua
4.4	Recuperación de las Islas Malvinas
1.5	Día del Trabajador
25.5	Fundación del Primer Gobierno Nacional
20.6	Día de la Bandera
9.7	Día de la Independencia
17.8	Muerte del General San Martín
12.10	Descubrimiento de América
8.12	Inmaculada Concepción de la Virgen María
25.12	Navidad

(RCH) Chile
1.1	Año Nuevo
25.3	Viernes Santo
27.3	Pascua
1.5	Día del Trabajo
21.5	Combate Naval de Iquique
23.5	Corpus Christi
15.8	Asunción de la Virgen
18.9	Fiestas Patrias
19.9	Día del Ejército
12.10	Día de la Hispanidad
1.11	Todos los Santos
8.12	Inmaculada Concepción
25.12	Navidad

(ROK) Korea
1.1	New Year's Day
1.3	Independence Movement Day
5.4	Arbor Day
5.5	Children's Day
15.5	Buddha's Birthday
6.6	Memorial Day
17.7	Constitution Day
15.8	Independence Day
18.9	Chuseok
3.10	National Foundation Day
25.12	Christmas Day

(S) Sverige
1.1	Nyårsdagen
6.1	Trettondedag jul
25.3	Långfredagen
27.3	Påskdagen
28.3	Annandag påsk
1.5	Första maj
5.5	Kristi himmelsfärds dag
15.5	Pingstdagen
16.5	Annandag pingst
25.6	Midsommardagen
5.11	Alla helgons dag
25.12	Juldagen
26.12	Annandag jul

(UK) United Kingdom
1.1	New Year's Day
3.1	Public Holiday
4.1	Public Holiday (Scotland only)
17.3	Saint Patrick's Day (Northern Ireland only)
25.3	Good Friday
27.3	Easter Sunday
28.3	Easter Monday (except Scotland)
2.5	May Bank Holiday
30.5	Spring Bank Holiday
12.7	Battle of the Boyne Day (Northern Ireland only)
1.8	Summer Bank Holiday (Scotland only)
29.8	Summer Bank Holiday (except Scotland)
25.12	Christmas Day
26.12	Boxing Day
27.12	Public Holiday

(USA) United States
1.1	New Year's Day
17.1	Martin Luther King Day
21.2	President's Day
27.3	Easter Sunday
30.5	Memorial Day
4.7	Independence Day
5.9	Labor Day
10.10	Columbus Day
11.11	Veterans' Day
24.11	Thanksgiving Day
25.12	Christmas Day

(ZA) South Africa
1.1	New Year's Day
21.3	Human Rights Day
25.3	Good Friday
27.3	Easter Sunday
28.3	Family Day
27.4	Freedom Day
1.5	Workers' Day
2.5	Public Holiday
16.6	Youth Day
9.8	National Women's Day
24.9	Heritage Day
16.12	Day of Reconciliation
25.12	Christmas Day
26.12	Day of Goodwill

Some international holidays may be subject to change.

01–04.2006

YEAR PLANNER

JANUARY	FEBRUARY	MARCH	APRIL
1 Su	1 We	1 We	1 Sa
WEEK 1	2 Th	2 Th	2 Su
2 Mo	3 Fr	3 Fr	**WEEK 14**
3 Tu	4 Sa	4 Sa	3 Mo
4 We	5 Su ◑	5 Su	4 Tu
5 Th	**WEEK 6**	**WEEK 10**	5 We ◐
6 Fr ◐	6 Mo	6 Mo ◐	6 Th
7 Sa	7 Tu	7 Tu	7 Fr
8 Su	8 We	8 We	8 Sa
WEEK 2	9 Th	9 Th	9 Su
9 Mo	10 Fr	10 Fr	**WEEK 15**
10 Tu	11 Sa	11 Sa	10 Mo
11 We	12 Su	12 Su	11 Tu
12 Th	**WEEK 7**	**WEEK 11**	12 We
13 Fr	13 Mo ○	13 Mo	13 Th ○
14 Sa ○	14 Tu	14 Tu ○	14 Fr
15 Su	15 We	15 We	15 Sa
WEEK 3	16 Th	16 Th	16 Su
16 Mo	17 Fr	17 Fr	**WEEK 16**
17 Tu	18 Sa	18 Sa	17 Mo
18 We	19 Su	19 Su	18 Tu
19 Th	**WEEK 8**	**WEEK 12**	19 We
20 Fr	20 Mo	20 Mo	20 Th
21 Sa	21 Tu ◑	21 Tu	21 Fr ◑
22 Su ◑	22 We	22 We ◑	22 Sa
WEEK 4	23 Th ○	23 Th	23 Su
23 Mo	24 Fr	24 Fr	**WEEK 17**
24 Tu	25 Sa	25 Sa	24 Mo
25 We	26 Su	26 Su	25 Tu
26 Th	**WEEK 9**	**WEEK 13**	26 We
27 Fr	27 Mo	27 Mo	27 Th ●
28 Sa	28 Tu ●	28 Tu	28 Fr
29 Su ●		29 We ●	29 Sa
WEEK 5		30 Th	30 Su
30 Mo		31 Fr	
31 Tu			

05–08.2006

MAY	JUNE	JULY	AUGUST
WEEK 18	1 Th	1 Sa	1 Tu
1 Mo	2 Fr	2 Su	2 We ◐
2 Tu	3 Sa ◐	**WEEK 27**	3 Th
3 We	4 Su	3 Mo ◐	4 Fr
4 Th	**WEEK 23**	4 Tu	5 Sa
5 Fr ◐	5 Mo	5 We	6 Su
6 Sa	6 Tu	6 Th	**WEEK 32**
7 Su	7 We	7 Fr	7 Mo
WEEK 19	8 Th	8 Sa	8 Tu
8 Mo	9 Fr	9 Su	9 We ○
9 Tu	10 Sa	**WEEK 28**	10 Th
10 We	11 Su ○	10 Mo	11 Fr
11 Th	**WEEK 24**	11 Tu ○	12 Sa
12 Fr	12 Mo	12 We	13 Su
13 Sa ○	13 Tu	13 Th	**WEEK 33**
14 Su	14 We	14 Fr	14 Mo
WEEK 20	15 Th	15 Sa	15 Tu
15 Mo	16 Fr	16 Su	16 We ◑
16 Tu	17 Sa	**WEEK 29**	17 Th
17 We	18 Su ◑	17 Mo ◑	18 Fr
18 Th	**WEEK 25**	18 Tu	19 Sa
19 Fr	19 Mo	19 We	20 Su
20 Sa ◑	20 Tu	20 Th	**WEEK 34**
21 Su	21 We	21 Fr	21 Mo
WEEK 21	22 Th	22 Sa	22 Tu
22 Mo	23 Fr	23 Su	23 We ●
23 Tu	24 Sa	**WEEK 30**	24 Th
24 We	25 Su ●	24 Mo	25 Fr
25 Th	**WEEK 26**	25 Tu ●	26 Sa
26 Fr	26 Mo	26 We	27 Su
27 Sa ●	27 Tu	27 Th	**WEEK 35**
28 Su	28 We	28 Fr	28 Mo
WEEK 22	29 Th	29 Sa	29 Tu
29 Mo	30 Fr	30 Su	30 We
30 Tu		**WEEK 31**	31 Th ◐
31 We		31 Mo	

09–12.2006

SEPTEMBER	OCTOBER	NOVEMBER	DECEMBER
1 Fr	1 Su	1 We	1 Fr
2 Sa	**WEEK 40**	2 Th	2 Sa
3 Su	2 Mo	3 Fr	3 Su
WEEK 36	3 Tu	4 Sa	**WEEK 49**
4 Mo	4 We	5 Su ○	4 Mo
5 Tu	5 Th	**WEEK 45**	5 Tu ○
6 We	6 Fr	6 Mo	6 We
7 Th ○	7 Sa ○	7 Tu	7 Th
8 Fr	8 Su	8 We	8 Fr
9 Sa	**WEEK 41**	9 Th	9 Sa
10 Su	9 Mo	10 Fr	10 Su
WEEK 37	10 Tu	11 Sa	**WEEK 50**
11 Mo	11 We	12 Su ◑	11 Mo
12 Tu	12 Th	**WEEK 46**	12 Tu ◑
13 We	13 Fr	13 Mo	13 We
14 Th ◑	14 Sa ◑	14 Tu	14 Th
15 Fr	15 Su	15 We	15 Fr
16 Sa	**WEEK 42**	16 Th	16 Sa
17 Su	16 Mo	17 Fr	17 Su
WEEK 38	17 Tu	18 Sa	**WEEK 51**
18 Mo	18 We	19 Su	18 Mo
19 Tu	19 Th	**WEEK 47**	19 Tu
20 We	20 Fr	20 Mo ●	20 We ●
21 Th	21 Sa	21 Tu	21 Th
22 Fr ●	22 Su ●	22 We	22 Fr
23 Sa	**WEEK 43**	23 Th	23 Sa
24 Su	23 Mo	24 Fr	24 Su
WEEK 39	24 Tu	25 Sa	**WEEK 52**
25 Mo	25 We	26 Su	25 Mo
26 Tu	26 Th	**WEEK 48**	26 Tu
27 We	27 Fr	27 Mo	27 We ◐
28 Th	28 Sa	28 Tu ◐	28 Th
29 Fr	29 Su ◐	29 We	29 Fr
30 Sa ◐	**WEEK 44**	30 Th	30 Sa
	30 Mo		31 Su
	31 Tu		

ADDRESSES AND NOTES

ADDRESSES AND NOTES